How to

TENNIS

Written by Charles S. Hellman
Illustrated by Robert A. Tiritilli

Raquette and Fuzzy
bring you a <u>simple</u> introduction to
tennis scoring... and more.

ISBN 0-935938-50-8

How to Score
TENNIS

"I'm Raquette"

"Hi, I'm Fuzzy"

"Fuzzy, Raquette and others
will be helping you "Volley" your way
in understanding how to keep score!"

Dear Fuzzy and Raquette:
I can't for the life of me figure out why tennis scoring is so strange. First you get fifteen, then thirty, and just when you think there's a pattern developing, the next point is called forty. And then the term "LOVE" pops into the score. I've been asking all the "experts," but they all just shrug and mumble. What do you say, Fuzzy and Raquette?
—George, Palm Springs, CA

George:
There's a reason for everything, old boy—not necessarily a good reason, but an explanation just the same. Tennis scoring has its derivation in medieval numerology. The number 60 was considered to be a "good" or "complete" number back then, in about the same way you'd consider a million to be a nice round figure today. The medieval version of tennis, therefore, was based on 60—the four points were 15, 30, 45 (which was later altered to 40) and 60, or game.
Cheers,
Fuzzy and Raquette

P.S. – On the next page is a letter that explains the term "LOVE".

Dear Fuzzy and Raquette:
**OK… answer this one. Why does *"LOVE"*
mean nothing in scoring tennis? – June,
Chicago, Il**

June:
*There seems to be a universal misconception
that the equally puzzling "love," or zero, is
derived from the French l'oeuf, "egg," or, by
extension, goose egg or zero. Actually, it comes
from the idea of playing for love, rather than
money—the implication being that one who
scores zero consistently can only be motivated
by a true love of the game. Tennis originated in
the 12th or 13th century someplace in France,
where it was called jeu de paume ("palm
game"). It seems to have derived its present
appellation from the French habit of called
"tenez!" before serving.*
Smiles,
Fuzzy and Raquette

Tennis originated in in France, where it was called jeu de paume ("palm game").

Court tennis has been played since the 13th century. The progression from court tennis, which used an unresilient sheepskin ball filled with sawdust, sand, or wool, to lawn tennis depended upon invention of a ball that would bounce.

Lawn tennis caught on quickly in Great Britain, and soon the All England Croquet Club at Wimbledon held the first world tennis championship in 1877. This event became the famous Wimbledon Tournament for the British National Championship and was restricted to male players.

In 1884, Wimbledon inaugurated a women's championship. Soon the game of tennis became popular in many parts of the British Empire, especially in Australia.

Tennis spread to the United States and became the sport that originally built Palm Springs. Probably the first pioneer who helped to establish the city of Palm Springs as a world renowned "watering place" for tennis was Charlie Farrell. In 1931 at the height of his prominence as a "Hollywood Film Star", he was in need of a vacation from his exhausting schedule of making one motion picture after another.

Farrell escaped to Palm Springs, and at the advice of Janet Gaynor, stopped at Harold Hick's real estate shack on the outskirts of town. At that time Palm Springs consisted of two big hotels —the Desert Inn on Palm Canyon Drive (now the site of the Desert Inn Fashion Plaza) and the El Mirador Hotel. When told of a 200 acre parcel available about a half-mile from the El Mirador for $30.00 an acre, Farrell was skeptical due to its distance from the center of town.

He was saved from one of the biggest mistakes of his life when his actor/tennis playing buddy Ralph Bellamy yelled, *"If it isn't underwater, buy it!"* and buy it they did. Bellamy and Farrell were dedicated tennis buffs. In those days Palm Springs boasted only two public tennis courts. The new landowners decided to build two courts on a portion of their 200 acres which fronted on the dirt road, Indian Avenue.

As the demand for court time increased, especially from their countless Hollywood friends, they gradually added club facilities and more courts. And so it began. Bette Davis, Ginger Rogers, Joan Crawford, Marlene Dietrich, Clark Cable and Errol Flynn were just a few who retreated to the quiet desert, eager to get away from their adoring fans. That was the launching of the famous and world-renowned Palm Springs Racquet Club.

Tennis Quiz

Fuzzy says, *"Knowledge is power."* Maybe not Andy Roddick's power, but perhaps some of what made Maria Sharapova so successful. Raquette loves this fun quiz which covers the basics of tennis, such as positioning, scoring, serves, forehands, and backhands. They think you'll have fun trying this quiz and probably pick up a few useful tips, too.

1Q: How high is the net at its center?
   A. 29 inches
   B. 36 inches
   C. 40 inches

2Q: The line that runs parallel to the net and is farthest from the net is called the
   A. Back line
   B. Foul line
   C. Baseline

3Q: The best way to hold the ball in Fuzzy's tossing hand is:
   A. Between his thumb and little finger
   B. Against his palm
   C. By the fingertips of all five fingers

4Q. Which serve will kick highest when it hits the opponent's court?

    A. Slice

    B. Hook

    C. Twist

5Q: While serving the ball, Raquette swings and misses the ball completely,

    A. It's a fault.

    B. It's a let.

    C. It's a missed serve, unless she catches the toss.

6Q: In each point of a match, how many chances does Fuzzy get to make a serve go in (not counting re-tries because the ball nicks the net on its way in)?

    A. One

    B. Two

    C. Three

7Q; Who won the men's single 2013 Wimbledon?

    A. Rafael Nadel

    B. Novak Djokovic

    C. Andy Murray

8Q: In the middle of a point, just as Raquette is about to hit a ball, Fuzzy yells, "Don't miss!" She misses and claims Fuzzy distracted her. What's the result?

    A. Fuzzy wins the point.

    B. Fuzzy loses the point

    C. Fuzzy replays the point.

9Q: Which of the following could not be the final set score?

    A. 6-5

    B. 6-0

    C. 9-7

10Q: What's Raquette's score, if she has won two points in a game?

    A. Love

    B. 15

    C. 30

Answers!

1-B, 2-C,3-C,4-C,5-C,6-A,7-C,8-B, 9-A,10-C

Tennis Etiquette

Fuzzy and Raquette prefer tennis over many other sports because they don't need to find another player in order to have a game. There are players who have a hard time getting a game, either because they are not any fun to have on the court and/or they do not understand the rules of the game.

Tennis has its official rules and also has *The Code of Tennis*, the unofficial rules of good tennis sportsmanship. Any serious player should take the time to read both. Fuzzy has seen all too many players argue adamantly about a rule on which they were completely wrong. Players who don't understand the rules, or worse, The Code, are more likely to experience a shrinking pool of opponents.

Tennis Scoring

Tennis is a fun game. When one is just learning the game, hitting the ball back and forth is fun, but as the players' proficiency in the game increases, they won't be content just hitting the ball over the net. Eventually, they would like to enjoy the game more by utilizing tennis scoring.

Tennis scoring takes a little getting used to. Generally, people play a set, or best out of three sets. Each set consists of a number of games.

We will show you how this Mumbo - Jumbo -- 15-30 -- blah, blah, blah -- LOVE --- blah --- works.

To put the tennis scoring system as simply as possible, one must win:

- Four points to win a game.
- Six games to win a set.
- Two sets to win a match.

By winning a coin toss or a spin of the racquet, the winner gets to choose one of the following:

- Serve
- Receive serve
- Choose an end of the court
- Have loser choose

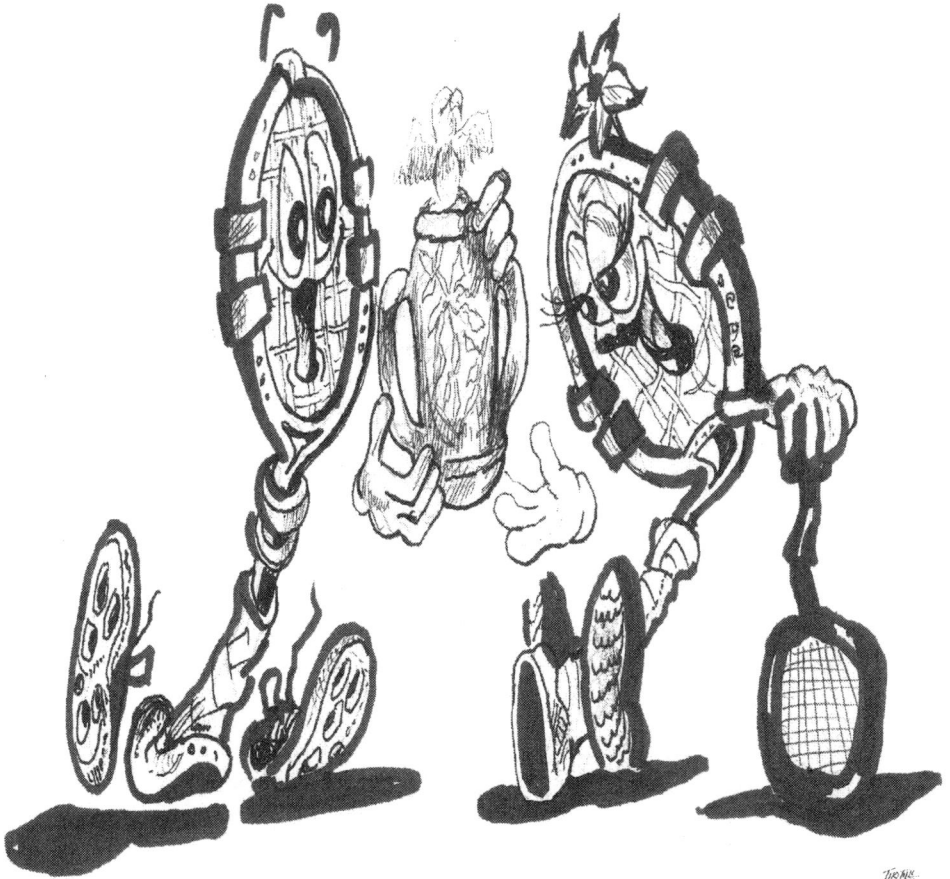

If **Fuzzy** wins the toss, he can choose which end of the court he wants to defend. The game begins as **Raquette** serves over the net to the opposite court from behind the baseline between the right singles' sideline and the center mark.

Raquette's serve must be struck before the ball bounces, and it must land in the serving box diagonally opposite her. Raquette gets two chances to get a serve in. If she misses both, she loses the point. If a serve that is otherwise good, nicks the net on its way in, is redone (Let Ball).

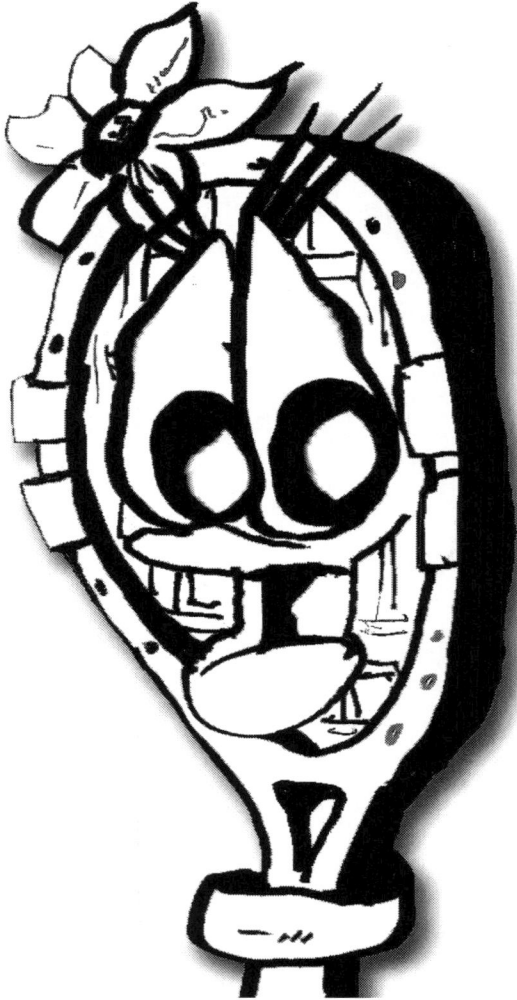

Fuzzy must return the ball after exactly one bounce, into any part of Raquette's singles court.

Raquette and Fuzzy must then return the ball after no more than one bounce, into one another's singles court until one of them misses.

A tennis game, when not prolonged by a tie, is played to four points, designated by the terms 15, 30, 40, and game, with zero points being referred to by the term love (possibly derived from the French word for egg, I'oeuf, referring to the physical appearance of the number zero).

Scoring is identical in the singles and doubles' games. In tennis competition, the score of the server is always given first. Typical scores at stages of a given tennis game might be "love-15" or "40-30." Like a lot of things, it sounds a lot more complicated on paper than it is in real life.

The first person to win six games wins the set; the smallest number of games in a set would be six (if the score were 6-0). However, to win a set you must win by two games, so if the score is 5-5, the set will go on till someone wins by two (7-5, 8-6,etc.), kind of like extra innings in baseball.

Tennis matches are usually the best two out of three sets or the best three out of five sets. A tie breaker is often employed if a set becomes tied at 6-6.

After reaching deuce, the player who can win the game on the next point is said to have the advantage, while a subsequent tied score is always called deuce. (A system referred to as "no-ad" is sometimes employed in which the winner of the point following the first deuce wins the game).

Tennis Scoring Con't

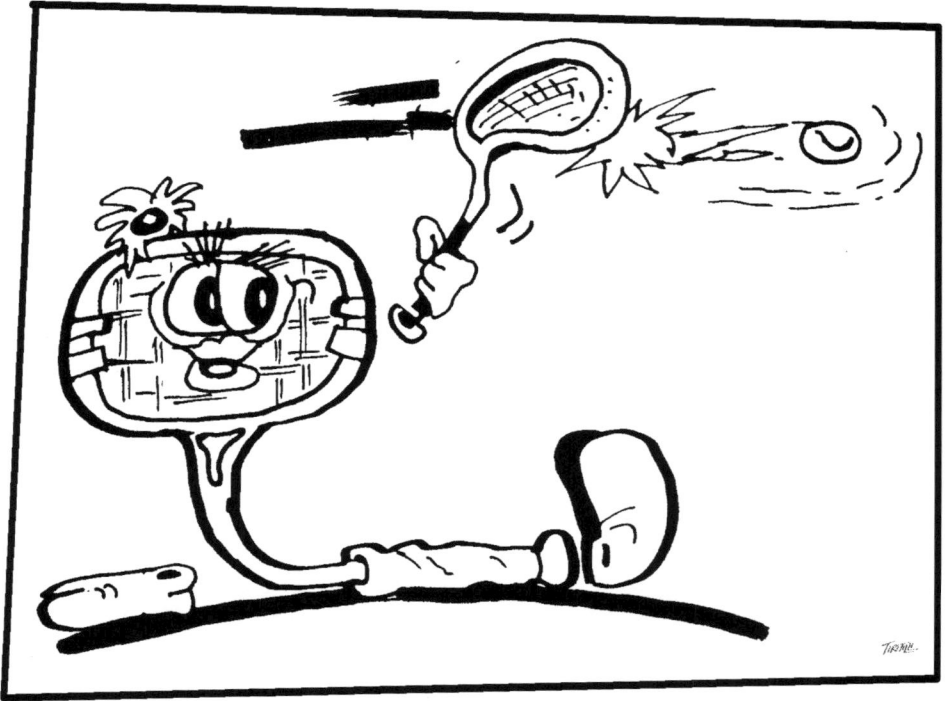

Players must win six games to win the set, but they must win by at least two games. Thus, if a set becomes tied at 5-5, at least 7 game victories are required to win the set.

This is where scoring a tiebreaker becomes difficult. A tiebreaker is generally played to 7 points, but because it too must be won by at least two points, it may be extended.

Winner of a tiebreaker is recorded as having won the set 7-6, regardless of the point total achieved in the tiebreaker. In many competitions, players play a tiebreaker if the set is tied 6-6 instead of fighting it out for a two-game lead.

With traditional scoring, games can go back and forth from deuce to ad over and over. The "No Ad" variation on the scoring within games allows for a game to be won by a margin of one point. Instead of "15," "30," and "40" used to note points, players may use "1," "2," "3." At "3 all" the receiver may choose whether to receive in the left right service box. The winner of that point wins the game.

WOW! So that's how they came up with this scoring system? Hum!

I guess way back in medieval numerology days, tennis did have its origin. The number "60" was considered to be a "good" or "complete" number back then, in about the same way you'd consider 100 to be a nice round figure today. Maybe that's why we have 60 minutes in an hour.

The medieval version of tennis, therefore, was based on 60 - the four points were 15, 30, 45 (which was abbreviated to 40) and 60, or game.

15 – 1st Point

30 – 2nd Point

45 – 3rd Point

60 – 4th Point/Game

There is certainly a reason... and not necessarily a good reason, but a reason just the same. Either way, it's how this glorious game is played and maybe serendipity came into play or not--- this is how we score the game of tennis.

43

You at least got the hard part of tennis over with... learning how to keep score!

Now comes the easy part...

PLAY!
&
ENJOY!

Other

TENNIS

Books

Tennis Humor is available on Amazon.com

Adventures in SportsLand

The Tennis Bully

The Tennis Bully is available on Amazon.com

Surprise!

Printed in Great Britain
by Amazon